WATER FOR AFRICA THROUGH LEADERSHIP AND INSTITUTIONAL SUPPORT (WALIS)

SIX MONTH WORKPLAN

OCTOBER 1, 2015 TO MARCH 31, 2016

Program Title: Water for Africa through Leadership and Institutional Support (WALIS)

Sponsoring USAID Office: Bureau for Africa's Office of Sustainable Development (AFR/SD)

Date of Publication: October 31, 2015

CONTENTS

ACRONYMS & ABBREVIATIONS

AFR/SD	USAID Bureau for Africa – Sustainable Development
AfWA	Africa Water Association
AMCOW	African Ministers' Council on Water
ANEW	African Civil Society Network on Water and Sanitation
COP	Chief of Party
DRC	Democratic Republic of Congo
FABRI	USAID-funded Further Advancing the Blue Revolution Project
IRC	International Rescue Committee
JMP	Joint Monitoring Programme
JSR	Joint Sector Review
KM	Knowledge Management
M&E	Monitoring and evaluation
NGO	Non-Governmental Organization
PSU	Project Support Unit
RWSN	Rural Water Supply Network
STTA	Short term technical assistance
TAMIS	Technical and Administrative Management Information System
TBD	To be determined
TOCO	Task Order Contracting Officer
TOCOR	Task Order Contracting Officer Representative
TRG	Training Resources Group, Inc.
UNICEF	United Nations International Children's Emergency Fund
USAID	United States Agency for International Development
WADI	USAID's Water and Development IDIQ
WALIS	Water for Africa through Leadership and Institutional Support
WASH	Water, Sanitation and Hygiene
WHO	World Health Organization
WSP	Water and Sanitation Program

INTRODUCTION TO WALIS

Despite significant progress made through donor and NGO investments over the past thirty years, a large percentage of Africans still lack access to clean water and proper sanitation. The data that African countries report to the Joint Monitoring Programme (JMP) often masks significant disparities between rural/urban populations and between rich and poor. These statistics also fail to capture the impact of poor water and sanitation access on women and girls who bear the primary responsibility for collecting and managing household water supplies and hygiene. They also face greater health and safety issues when confronted with limited access to sanitation facilities.

Many African countries are testing and applying different approaches to improve access to clean, safe water and improved sanitation. These offer good examples of market-oriented and public-private partnership approaches that can help countries address specific water, sanitation and hygiene (WASH) challenges. Unfortunately, too often these examples and the lessons they generate get little notice or dissemination outside the country or city where they take place. Based on our experience, replicating successful WASH models requires two key ingredients: (1) wide availability of information about the approach and how it was developed (i.e. not just a simple success story); and (2) the local capacity to understand and adapt the approach to the different political, social, economic and environmental conditions reflected in the targeted country or region.

WALIS GOALS AND MISSION

The DAI team will work with AFR/SD to make WALIS a flexible support platform that fosters and promotes a culture of inquiry among African regional and national WASH partners and strengthens WASH programs and programming. By maintaining a strong focus on "why" – namely delivering improved access to safe water and improved sanitation for all Africans – we will work with USAID and African regional organizations and networks to:

- Strengthen a cadre of WASH leaders who will champion the use of data and evidence to drive changes in national policies and practices that deliver improved sanitation and safe water.
- Build demand for better data collection systems and objective analyses that will underpin further improvements in WASH policies, governance and programs.
- Strengthen the capture, dissemination and application of WASH lessons learned and best practices.

WALIS STRATEGIC APPROACH

WALIS will address this challenge by cultivating and reinforcing a culture of inquiry based on the scientific method (see Figure 1).

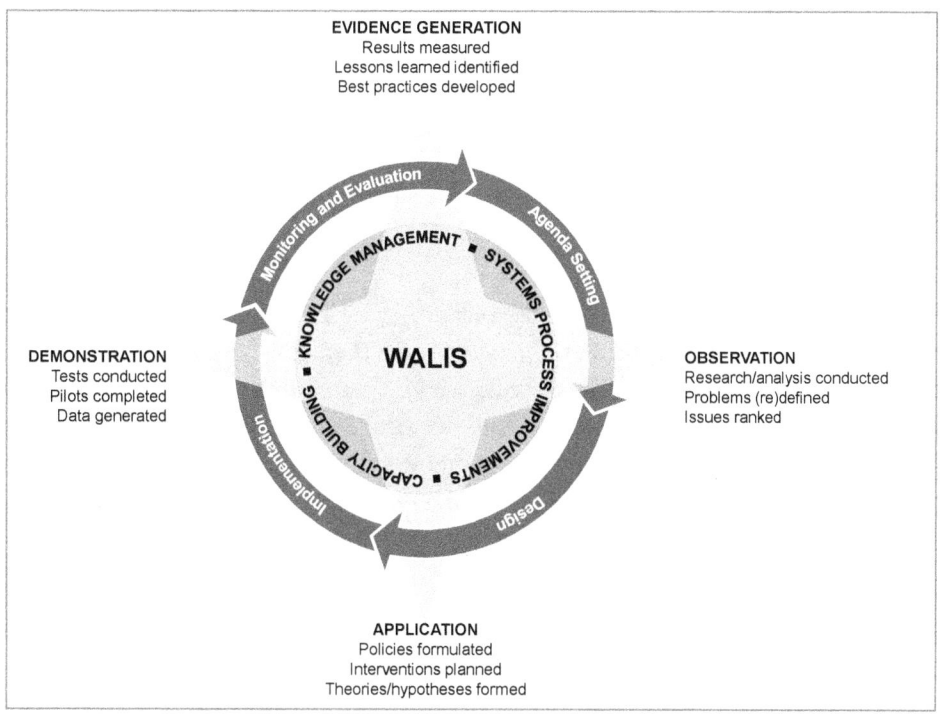

The scientific method offers an ongoing process – observation, design, testing and evidence-generation - that lends itself to refinement of policies and the generation of tested approaches that can be scaled up for impact. It begins with observations to shape approaches and hypotheses, which are then tested through pilot initiatives. The analysis of these tests/pilots leads to more observations and evidence that in turn, contributes to the further refinement of policies, strategies and plans, in an iterative process.

By strengthening the capacity of African regional organizations and their country members to monitor, evaluate and apply knowledge and data when developing strategies and making programming decisions, we will reinforce a culture of inquiry that delivers improved access to clean water and sanitation.

IDENTIFYING DEMAND FOR WALIS SERVICES – OUR 6 MONTH WORK PLAN

This initial work plan will focus on effectively engaging with USAID's AFR/SD and Water teams, USAID field missions in Africa, African regional partners (i.e. AfWA, AMCOW and ANEW), and selected national partner representatives. We will use this period to establish baselines, and identify, design and launch activities that respond to early priorities identified by USAID and regional and national partners. WALIS COP Richard Pollard and team members will recommend to USAID specific areas of assistance, country-level research and studies, and the types of activities to prioritize with each regional organization and network after completing consultations planned for the WALIS roadshow discussed further below.

In the interim, the following section outlines our approach for engaging with partners, the roll-out of WALIS, and initial proposed activities under each task.

PRIORITIZING WHERE TO WORK

USAID has prioritized 15 countries in Africa for investments in WASH and water resources management related to food security. USAID divided these into Tier 1 and Tier 2 priorities under its Water and Development Strategy. Table 1 below lists these countries, the level of water funding as shown in the 2015 and 2016 Congressional Budget Justifications, and summarizes major WASH efforts. This table shows the significant expansion of USAID's WASH portfolio in Africa over the past five years. Currently, five countries (Ethiopia, Ghana, Kenya, Senegal and Tanzania) have either just launched, or are about to launch, significant new WASH projects, and another four countries (Malawi, Nigeria, Rwanda and Uganda) are developing new WASH projects.

Table 1: USAID Programming for WASH in Africa

	Country	Current USAID Programs	Approximate Annual Funding Levels		Notes
			2015	2016	
Tier 1	Ethiopia	Lowland Water, Sanitation and Hygiene project	$6,952[1]	$3,485[2]	Pending award. 4 year, $23M (approximate) value) – rural WASH in Somali, Afar and SNNPR provinces
	Kenya	Integrated WASH project	$5,730[2]	$4,166[2]	Recently awarded. $50 million, 5 year program (2015 – 2020) focused on improving WASH in 9 counties of Kenya
	Liberia	Municipal Water Project	$5,338	$5,070	Ongoing. 2010 – 2014 with option to extend 2 years. Focused on improving water supplies in three secondary cities – Robertsport, Sanniquellie and Voinjama.
	Nigeria		$3,360	$2,256[2]	New project under development
	South Sudan	South Sudan Rural Water, Sanitation and Hygiene (SSRWASH) Project	$9,700	$7,245	Four year, $58M project focused on rural WASH in S. Sudan. Not awarded and assistance to S. Sudan halted due to political/conflict crisis
Tier 2	DRC		$2,500[3]	$0	No known USAID WASH project
	Ghana	Water and Sanitation project	$5,570[2]	$3,412	Awarded 2014. X year, $14.2M project. Also receives support under the West Africa Water Initiative (WAWI)
	Malawi		$19[3]	$537[3]	NewWASH project under preparation
	Mali		$1,640	$1,441	Receives support under West Africa Water Initiative
	Mozambique		$1,841[3]	$1,889[2]	No known USAID WASH project
	Rwanda	Water and Sanitation Infrastructure and Capacity Building Activity	$1,686[3]	$839[3]	New project under development.
	Senegal	Projet Assainissement, Changement de Comportement et Eau pour le Sénégal (ACCES)	$1,500[2]	N/A	Pending award. $22M 5 year project to expand WASH access in the six regions of Senegal - Ziguinchor, Sedhiou, Kolda, Kedougou, Tambacounda and Matam.
	Tanzania	Water Resources Integration Development Initiative (WARIDI)	$5,096[3]	$5,253[2]	Pending award. Approximately $50M five year program focused on improving WASH and water resources mgt in the Rufiji and Wami-Ruvu river basins in Southern Tanzania
	Uganda	Sanitation project	$6,178[3]	$4,394[3]	Under development. 5-year, approximately $31M project to accelerate sustainable improvement in quality, access and supply of water and sanitation services, and improve hygiene behaviors in Uganda.
	Zambia	School WASH program (SPLASH)	$1,696[3]	$3,897[2]	5 year $20M 2014 – 2019 focused on improving sanitation and hygiene t in 616 primary schools in Eastern Province of Zambia

[1] Food for Peace and/or Global Health Funding
[2] DA and GH blend
[3] Global Health

At the suggestion of USAID that WALIS focus more effort on Tier 2 countries (but not preclude Tier 1 countries), we have put together Table 2 to highlight specific WASH-related indicators. The data shown was sourced from the World Health Organization (WHO) and from the JMP. It shows that while many countries have made significant progress in expanding access to safe water sources over the past decade, access to improved sanitation still lags significantly in some countries such as Ghana, Tanzania and Uganda. What this table also shows is that in spite of advances in expanding access to safe water, child mortality from diarrheal disease remains very high in most countries.

Table 2: WASH Indicator for Selected African Countries

Country	Population (Millions) 2014	Access to Water 2015 JMP	Access to Sanitation 2015 JMP	Diarrheal Deaths 2004	< 5 Mortality due to diarrhea 2004
DRC	69.3	52	29	205/1000	18.1%
Ghana	26.4	89	15	112/1000	12.2%
Malawi	16.8	90	41	175/1000	18.1%
Mali	15.8	77	25	219/1000	18.3%
Mozambique	26.5	51	21	152/1000	16.5%
Rwanda	12.1	76	62	203/1000	18.5%
Senegal	14.5	78	48	137/1000	17.1%
Tanzania	50.8	56	16	126/1000	16.8%
Uganda	38.8	74	19	138/1000	17.2%

Although WALIS will need to be demand driven, the above brief analysis suggests that WALIS should focus its efforts on countries such as the DRC, Liberia, Mali and Mozambique where USAID either does not have a significant WASH program already in-place, or where programs are nearing completion (i.e. Liberia).

ENGAGING WITH KEY PARTNERS

In the first six months of operation, the WALIS team will engage with three different partner groups to build ownership in the project and solicit their inputs into the project's planning and priority setting processes. We also will use these engagement efforts to identify where to leverage WALIS' resources and forge strategic partnerships that will help expand the reach and impact of WALIS activities and strengthen the foundation for long-term success and sustainability. The three groups are:

USAID. We will engage with AFR/SD, the USAID Water Team, and with some USAID missions in Africa to inform them about WALIS, identify an initial set of priority countries and activities, and discuss USAID's interest and need for a research-on-demand facility that can draw on existing literature to answer questions raised by USAID staff about lessons learned and best practices in WASH policies, strategies and approaches.

Regional WASH Partners and Donors. The WALIS team will start by tapping into their existing relationships with both AfWA and AMCOW leadership as well as donors such as WSP, UNICEF, World Bank and the Gates Foundation to inform them about WALIS and potential areas of work and collaboration. The team will also reach out to and forge working relationships with other important organizations such as African Civil Society Network on Water and Sanitation (ANEW), the Rural Water Supply Network (RWSN), African Water Operators Partnership (AWOP), and the Sanitation and Water for All (SWA) initiative to seek their input about WALIS priorities.

Selected National Governments and Stakeholders. The WALIS team will use regional events to engage with participating representatives from national governments, share information about WALIS, and hold one-on-one and small group discussions with WASH champions from selected Tier 1 and Tier 2 countries about national priorities and needs in relation to WALIS's four task areas.

Our engagement will be initiated in two main phases. The first phase will be a kickoff workshop that will be held on November 19, 2015 at USAID. It will focus on informing USAID regional and technical specialists about the project and identify priority areas of interest and potential collaboration. The second phase will involve targeted project announcements and surveys to USAID missions in early 2016, culminating in a project roadshow that will provide opportunities for detailed discussions and joint planning with development partners in Western, Eastern, and Southern Africa.

PRIORITIZING PROJECT THEMATIC AREAS

African countries have significant and diverse information and technical needs as they struggle to improve access to safe water and improved sanitation. USAID has strategically and uniquely positioned WALIS to focus on a few specific areas – areas which have been often overlooked in order to address the immediate demands to improve water supplies and access to sanitation. In that regard, WALIS will focus on improving country and regional data and research and country capacity to use data and studies for evidence-based policy making and program planning. We will use the roadshow to identify regional institution, country and USAID mission priorities that can be addressed within the WALIS framework.

Nevertheless, we anticipate that sanitation and institutional strengthening will be significant areas of interest given that: (1) until recently few donors were investing in the institutional side of sanitation, and (2) many countries now recognize that getting households to invest in toilets is only the first step in lowering the incidence of diarrheal disease and its health and economic impacts. This will create secondary challenges such as the institutional, policy and operational foundation for the collection and treatment of human wastes.

The WALIS roadshow will provide the opportunity for the team to interview regional and host country partners to identify areas where WALIS can provide support that leads to better use of data and information in shaping policies, program plans and actions that deliver results.

The following activities will be implemented by the WALIS team to prioritize countries and thematic areas, reach out to stakeholders, and secure their engagement:

A. WALIS Marketing and Informational Material

DAI's marketing and publications department has been engaged to produce an informational kit of WALIS, including a brochure targeting institutional partners and a leaflet that can distributed to the general public during meetings and workshops. The materials include information about WALIS's goals and range of services, and will be tailored to each of the key target groups. This initial material will be supplemented with information on types of support mechanisms and USAID Missions buy-in opportunities for technical support, assessments and pilot activities after the initial project Roadshow.

B. USAID Kick-off Workshop

Sub-contractor TRG will be engaged to organize and moderate a workshop in Washington DC in early December (date to be determined in collaboration with the TOCOR). The workshop will convene DC-based USAID AFR/SD and Water team members along with WALIS management and partners to discuss the overall project vision, prioritization of countries and preliminary thematic areas. Feedback from this workshop will serve to hone marketing and informational materials as well as securing support from these teams for the implementation of the roadshow.

C. Participation in Key Events.

WALIS COP, Richard Pollard will attend the Sanitation Workshop in Dakar co-organized by the Further Advancing the Blue Revolution (FABRI) project and the Gates Foundation in January 2016, as well as the AfWA Congress that will be held in February in Nairobi. These events will provide opportunities to present the WALIS project to several African stakeholders, including AfWA, as well as USAID field staff. In keeping with the project's country engagement strategy, we will seek to interact with and identify champions from countries that represent a programmatic priority. In addition, the management team, including the Technical Activity Manager, will work with the Rural Water Supply Network (RWSN) to identify an additional event in the first quarter of 2016 presenting a good opportunity to interact with African stakeholders.

D. The WALIS Africa Roadshow.

The centerpiece of WALIS's engagement strategy, the WALIS Africa Roadshow will extend for about three weeks between the end of January and early February 2016 (specific dates to be discussed with TOCOR). The Roadshow will consist of three regional meetings involving African regional organizations, selected USAID regional and bilateral missions; and some of their host government counterparts. The proposed locations for these meetings are Dakar, Nairobi and Pretoria, where USAID has regional offices supporting West, East and Southern Africa, respectively. In these meetings, the WALIS management team, led by COP Pollard will provide an overview of WALIS, and engage participants in identifying specific demands and early needs that WALIS can support. We also will use these meetings to identify "champions for change" that we can involve in WALIS tasks and the design and implementation of demonstration and pilot activities. Senior Operations Manager, Rachel Tkachuk, will start organizing the logistical and administrative aspects of the Roadshow in close collaboration with the TOCOR. Concurrently, the Technical Activity Manager and Senior Program Director, Piers Cross, will reach out to regional partners and government counterparts to sell the event and secure participation. Partner representatives from Taoti, TRG, and Cloudburst will join the WALIS team to provide details on the operational tools available for the missions and other partners.

The following table presents operational details for the activities to be implemented to prioritize countries and thematic areas, reach out to stakeholders, and secure their engagement:

Table 3. Proposed activities to secure partner engagement and prioritize thematic areas on a demand-driven basis.

Illustrative Activities	Budget	Status	Start Date	End Date
Developing WALIS marketing and informational materials	$	Design	Nov 2015	Dec 2015
USAID kick-off workshop	$	Design	Dec 2015	Dec 2015
Participation in key water sector events in Africa	$	Design	Dec 2015	Mar 2016
WALIS Africa Roadshow	$	Design	Jan 2016	Feb 2016

SPECIFIC ACTIVITIES UNDER EACH TASK

In addition to the four activities designed to set the stage for a demand-driven implementation of WALIS, our team will advance some preliminary work under each of the contract Tasks. The activities presented below are intended to provide WALIS with fundamental baseline information and assessment that would be used to design specific activities for the month 7 to 12 Work Plan.

TASK 1: DEVELOPING, MONITORING, AND ANALYZING SOUND SECTOR DATA

Under this task, WALIS will strengthen the ability of regional and country partners, and USAID Missions to make informed decisions and better monitor and assess progress and impact of ongoing WASH activities and programs. The following are the activities our team will implement in the first six months:

A. Mapping of WASH Sector Data

WALIS's Monitoring and Evaluation Specialist will initiate a mapping of how WASH sector data is collected, reported and used for strategy and policy development and monitoring progress. The Monitoring and Evaluation Specialist will engage with AMCOW and its Monitoring and Evaluation Task Force members to explore where WALIS can support its efforts to harmonize and strengthen national monitoring and reporting systems for water and sanitation. This information will be used to develop an action plan to strengthen AMCOW's and individual countries' data collection and reporting mechanisms.

B. Knowledge Management Portal(s)

In the context of the project's Roadshow, Knowledge Management Specialist will organize one workshop with staff from AMCOW and AfWA and selected national counterparts to carry out a discovery and design process that will serve as a stepping stone to transform their websites into more useful portals for data and knowledge dissemination. This work will continue ongoing efforts under FABRI with AfWA.

C. Initial Donor Outreach

The COP and Senior Program Director will organize two meetings with at least two donors such as the World Bank, IRC, and UNICEF to establish a collaborative approach to helping countries improve their WASH sector data and analysis. Much attention has been given to improving sanitation and water sector monitoring in recent years by the donor and sector community; WALIS will seek to develop a coordinated approach that adds value to these efforts. The meetings will take place in the context of the project's Roadshow.

In addition, the team will meet with the Gates Foundation at the Sanitation Workshop in December to discuss potential areas of collaboration under WALIS, particularly on the implementation of pilot projects (see Task 2, Activity A below).

The following table presents operational details for the activities to be implemented as part of Task 1:

Table 4. Proposed activities under Task 1:

Illustrative Activities	Budget	Status	Start Date	End Date
Mapping of WASH sector data	$	Design	Nov 2015	Mar 2016
Knowledge management portal(s)	$	Design	Jan 2016	Mar 2016
Initial donor outreach	$	Design	Dec 2015	Mar 2016

Expected Outputs

- Mapping of AMCOW's and countries' WASH data collection and reporting systems completed.
- Workshop with AMCOW and other regional agencies such as AfWA on improving the website as an information portal completed and suggestions for improvements identified.
- Preliminary agreement to collaborate with at least one other donor to improve WASH sector data collection and analysis.

TASK 2: ENGAGING IN TARGETED RESEARCH AND PILOT ACTIVITIES AROUND IDENTIFIED SECTOR CONSTRAINTS

WALIS will design and support targeted assessments, tools and methods that will provide Bureaus, Missions, and country partners with actionable information to guide strategic, programming, or design decisions. In the first six months, the team will:

A. Identification and Preliminary Design of Pilot Activities

Following the WALIS Roadshow, review the research and pilot activities identified by regional and national government partners with AFR/SD, reach agreement on priorities and initiate their design.

B. Evaluate Replication of FABRI Activities

Provide continuing support to activities initiated under FABRI with selected water service providers to institute performance improvement plans, business plans and non-revenue water reduction programs, as well as for the fecal sludge management initiated with AfWA in collaboration with the Gates Foundation. We will use these as early experiences that WALIS can share with other water service providers across Africa.

C. Collaborate with RWSN to Augment Ongoing Work on Solar Pumping Technology in Rural Africa

The Rural Water Supply Network (RWSN) has initiated a robust research and development program to promote the use of solar energy for rural water supply pumping. WALIS will work closely with RWSN to identify areas for collaboration to continue and expand this work. One immediate area for possible joint work is the preparation of a field note on solar pumping that RWSN.

The following table presents operational details for the activities to be implemented as part of Task 2:

Table 5. Proposed activities under Task 2:

Illustrative Activities	Budget	Status	Start Date	End Date
Identification and preliminary design of pilot activities	$	Design	Jan 2016	Mar 2016
Evaluate replication of FABRI activities	$	Design	Dec 2015	Mar 2016
Identify areas for joint work on solar powered pumping with RWSN	$	Design	Jan 2016	Mar 2016

Expected Outputs

- Report summarizing initial research and pilot program priorities and potential donor partners. Specific opportunities for research/pilots in sanitation that support the Ngor Declaration identified.
- Collaboration agreement with Gates Foundation on sanitation.
- Collaboration agreement with RWSN on solar pumping and possibly others areas.

TASK 3: STRENGTHENING COUNTRY SYSTEMS TO DEVELOP INFORMED POLICY AND ENGAGE IN SECTOR PLANNING TOWARD SUSTAINABLE WASH SERVICES

WALIS will strengthen the capacity of regional institutions such as African Water Association (AfWA), the African Ministers Council on Water (AMCOW), the African Civil Society Network on Water and Sanitation (ANEW), and Sanitation and Water for All (SWA) to have a larger influence on African governments and WASH service providers in the region. In the first six months, the team will carry out the following:

A. Comparative Assessment of Joint Sector Review Process

In partnership with AMCOW and their respective member ministries, as well as with the Skat Foundation, initiate a comparative assessment of at least two country Joint Sector Review (JSR) processes that could be presented and discussed at Africa Water Week. This would build on and complement previous and ongoing JSR analytical work that is being carried out by the Skat Foundation and the World Bank Water and Sanitation Program (WSP).

The following table presents operational details for the activities to be implemented as part of Task 3:

Table 6. Proposed activities under Task 3:

Illustrative Activities	Budget	Status	Start Date	End Date
Evaluate the JSR or similar process in at least two (2) countries	$	Design	Jan 2016	Mar 2016

Expected Outputs

- Comparative assessment completed of two country Joint Sector Review processes with report to USAID and AMCOW
- Joint sessions or presentations (with Skat, WSP) on JSR analytical work and lessons learned at Africa Water Week and the RWSN Forum.

TASK 4: INCREASING THE CAPACITY REQUIRED TO SUPPORT IMPROVED COLLECTION AND USE OF SECTOR KNOWLEDGE

WALIS will identify, assess, develop, and train the regional institutions identified above in analysis, research, data collection, and policy reform to better disseminate information in the region among service providers and host governments. This may include working with other key donors, governments, and partners in a coordinated effort with these institutions to better leverage investments, sequence interventions, and complement efforts. In the first six months, the team will:

A. Launch Self-Guided Institutional Assessments for Regional Partners

Self-guided institutional assessments are a tool designed to help organizations identify institutional weaknesses and show how such analyses can be incorporated into business plan development. WALIS's Institutional Strengthening Specialist will use the context of the Roadshow to organize a training session with AMCOW, AfWA and the Africa Network on Water and Sanitation (ANEW) to present the tool and launch the first phase of training on the assessment. The training session will be followed up by a series of on-site and remote communications intended to support the proper implementation of the self-guided assessments. Upon finalization of the assessments, the Institutional Strengthening Specialist will prepare capacity building plans for each organization that would serve as the basis to roll out a program to improve data collection capacity.

The following table presents operational details for the activities to be implemented as part of Task 4:

Table 7. Proposed activities under Task 4:

Illustrative Activities	Budget	Status	Start Date	End Date
Launch first phase of training for guided self-assessments with AMCOW, AfWA, and ANEW	$	Design	Jan 2016	Mar 2016

Expected Outputs

- Self-guided institutional assessments for AfWA, AMCOW and ANEW launched, finalized and discussed with each organization. From these initial institutional strengthening plans drafted.

CROSS CUTTING THEMES

GENDER

In countries across Africa, the needs and interests of women are rarely represented adequately in the development of country WASH strategies, policies and programs. Numerous studies have highlighted this issue and recommended approaches to improve gender mainstreaming; however there is a dearth of good examples of how this can be done from planning through implementation. Current data collection and reporting mechanisms fail to capture the impact of poor water and sanitation access on women and girls who bear the primary responsibility for collecting and managing household water supplies and hygiene. They also face greater health and safety issues when confronted with limited access to sanitation facilities. In the first six months, the team will:

A) Conduct Comparative Analysis

We will mobilize our DC-based Gender Specialist by November 30, 2015 to conduct comparative analyses of different approaches for engaging women more integrally in the design, construction and management of WASH services, policies and strategies. As a key participant in the Roadshow, the Gender Specialist will identify mechanisms that regional partners could use for: (1) the collection of gender disaggregated baseline information, and (2) facilitating engagement of both women and men in project planning, design and implementation, and operations and monitoring.

B) Assess the Feasibility of a Gender Mainstreaming Task Force.

WALIS will work with interested regional partners to form Gender Mainstreaming Task Force that can work with national stakeholders to design and implement sanitation projects where gender is mainstreamed from the beginning through implementation and operation.

The following table presents operational details for the activities to be implemented as part of our Gender cross cutting theme:

Table 8. Proposed activities under Gender cross cutting theme:

Illustrative Activities	Budget	Status	Start Date	End Date
Conduct comparative analyses of approaches to engage women in the design of WASH activities	$	Design	Dec 2014	Mar 2016
Assess feasibility of forming a Gender Mainstreaming Task Force with regional partners	$	Design	Jan 2016	Mar 2016

Expected Outputs

- Comparative analyses report and strategy developed in collaboration with AfWA and AMCOW with priorities agreed with partners.
- Feasibility of Gender Mainstreaming Task Force determined and conceptual design developed in case it is feasible.

YOUTH

Similar to the challenges faced by women, youth remains largely in the periphery of the WASH Sector in Africa despite increasing efforts to change this reality. WALIS will support AMCOW's implementation of its Policy and Strategy for Mainstreaming Youth in Water and Sanitation Sector after a preliminary review of how we can get youth more engaged in helping set the WASH agenda and priorities. In the first six months, the team will:

A) Identify key priorities in collaboration with AMCOW

Senior Program Director Cross will lead a review of AMCOW's Policy and Strategy for Mainstreaming Youth in collaboration with Oseloka Zikora, Head of Communications and Nelson Gomonda, Project Manager (Monitoring & Reporting) starting in January 2016. The review will, inter alia, consider the project concepts portfolio of options for "early wins" to kick-start the strategy. The review will lead to the identification of priorities in the policy and project concepts that could be implemented with project support.

B) Assess viability of establishing a Young Professionals Development Grant Program

Building from our experience establishing a Young Professionals Development grant program under FABRI, our Technical Activity Manager will assess the viability of a similar effort under WALIS. The grant program would focus on attracting more young people to the WASH sector and deepening their skills and knowledge.

The following table presents operational details for the activities to be implemented as part of our Youth cross cutting theme:

Table 9. Proposed activities under Youth cross cutting theme:

Illustrative Activities	Budget	Status	Start Date	End Date
Identify key priorities and project concepts to kick-start implementation of AMCOW's Policy and Strategy for Mainstreaming Youth	$	Design	Jan 2016	Mar 2016
Assess viability of establishing a Young Professionals Development grant program with regional partners	$	Design	Jan 2016	Mar 2016

Expected Outputs

- AMCOW's Policy and Strategy for Mainstreaming Youth priorities identified and incorporated into WALIS second 6-month Work Plan.
- Viability of Young Professionals Development grant program determined and conceptual design developed in case it is viable.

MANAGEMENT STRUCTURE

WALIS' small team based out of the DAI home office provides an efficient management structure designed to ensure an immediate and flexible response to the needs of the AFR/SD Office in Washington, DC. A project support unit (PSU) consisting of the COP Richard Pollard, Senior Operations Manager Rachel Tkachuk, and the Technical Activity Manager (TBD) will oversee technical, financial and administrative tasks and will liaise with subcontractors to align short-term technical assistance resources and networks with project needs. The PSU's lean structure will allow for inclusion of additional personnel as new activities are identified by USAID or to accommodate specific mission buy-ins.

Chief of Party Richard Pollard will be the primary point of contact with the COR for all WALIS-related communication and relations, and will lead relationships with our subcontractors and with regional/national implementing partners across Africa. While the COP has not fully transitioned into the project, the Director of Environment, Miguel Baca, who oversees projects under this portfolio, will serve as the primary point of contact for the TOCOR and TOCO. By the end of Quarter 1 of the project, all team members will be on boarded, including COP Richard Pollard.

CHIEF OF PARTY MOBILIZATION AND TRANSITION

In order to build on the synergies between FABRI and WALIS, Chief of Party Richard Pollard will make a gradual transition between the two projects, becoming full time on WALIS in December 2015. This will ensure that the final major activities planned on FABRI over the next two months – including the Middle East and North Africa Network of Water Centers of Excellence Congress in Oman, a sanitation event in partnership with the Gates Foundation in Dakar, and a workshop on non-revenue water in Abidjan – are successfully executed and pave the way for both a smooth project closedown in March 2016 and sustained positive relationships with beneficiaries. The scope of WALIS provides several areas of technical overlap with FABRI, and these events will serve the dual purpose of introducing stakeholders and partners likely to continue collaboration under WALIS to the new project. The presence of Richard Pollard as the face of both should lessen confusion and provide assurance that critical support provided under FABRI will not be abandoned.

ADDITIONAL LTTA PERSONNEL

Upon contract signature, DAI immediately began recruiting for two additional long term positions, the Senior Operations Manager and Technical Activity Manager, who will both report directly to the COP and liaise with administrative and technical counterparts, respectively, in regional partner institutions. For the Senior Operations Manager, we have identified a strong internal candidate, Rachel Tkachuk, who is already intimately familiar with company systems, policies, and procedures, and we are excited that she brings a strong background in both grants administration and contractual compliance. We have also identified a well-qualified internal candidate for the Technical Activity Manager role, Anahit Gevorgyan. Finally, WALIS has recruited Piers Cross to serve as an intermittent Senior Program Director based full-time in Africa, although the project will not establish an office there. This regional presence will allow WALIS to improve communication with and visibility among local partners, increase responsiveness, and assist with tracking implementation progress and country and mission-specific needs.

SHORT-TERM TECHNICAL ASSISTANCE

As discussions with USAID and regional partners evolve into prioritized needs, technical expertise and surge capacity will be provided through the targeted use of short-term local and international advisors, identified either through DAI's own extensive networks or through those of WALIS' consortium members. As mentioned above, DAI's in-house recruitment resources allow for the rapid mobilization of personnel, both domestically and internationally. In order to achieve the results expected from the six month workplan, STTA needs have been identified and they are presented in Table 10 below:

Table 10: STTA Positions Identified for 6-Month Work Plan

STTA Position	Candidate	Partner	Expected Mobilization Date
Institutional Capacity Building / Facilitation	Redacted	Redacted	November 30, 2015
M&E Specialist	Redacted	Redacted	November 6, 2015
Gender Specialist	Redacted	Redacted	January 4, 2016

Knowledge Management Specialist	Redacted	Redacted	November 30, 2015
Web Developer	Redacted	Redacted	November 30, 2015

PARTNERS

DAI's core subcontractors for WALIS are Cloudburst, TRG, and Taoti. All small businesses with extensive prior experience engaging with USAID, they bring particular expertise in M&E, capacity building, and knowledge management, respectively, and WALIS will move to engage them in work plan and Performance Management Plan development by November 2015. TRG's input will inform technical activities supporting institutional strengthening for regional and national organizations, and Taoti and Cloudburst will be closely involved in the creation of tools responding to the needs of project partners. Table 11 presents our partner organizations and their clearly specified roles in WALIS.

Table 11: WALIS Consortium Rationale

Partner	Project Role/SOW
DAI—Prime Contractor	<ul><li>Project management, performance monitoring, quality control and compliance, general technical support.</li><li>Provides COP and field-based technical staff, short-term international and local technical experts, as well as all project operational staff in Washington, DC.</li><li>Coordinates with AFR/SD on project progress and contract compliance.</li><li>Ensures adherence to work plan, milestones, and M&E process, as well as contractual and financial compliance.</li></ul>
Cloudburst—WADI Subcontractor	<ul><li>Provides STTA M&E Specialist for Washington DC office team, as well as M&E and evaluation STTA specialists.</li><li>Conducts evaluations, including data gathering, impact, mid-term, longitudinal, outcome, formative, process, and case study evaluations in the United States and partner countries.</li></ul>
TRG—WADI Subcontractor	<ul><li>Provides STTA expertise for innovative training design and facilitation, with a specific focus on behavior change.</li><li>Conducts organizational assessments to identify institutional capacity building needs for regional and national-level partners.</li></ul>
Taoti—WADI Subcontractor	<ul><li>Provides STTA Communications/KM Specialist to develop innovative web-based tools for data capturing and sharing, including knowledge-sharing portals.</li><li>Technical support for knowledge dissemination and information technology-focused strengthening activities.</li></ul>

HOME OFFICE SUPPORT

To further support the WALIS project team, DAI provides numerous home office resources. A project management unit consisting of a project team director, project manager, and project associate will provide financial, operational, and contractual guidance, and will serve as the primary points of contact linking WALIS staff members to contracts, finance, procurement, IT, and human resources departments. DAI also offers dedicated in-house recruiters and systems that will allow for the rapid identification, vetting, and mobilization of short-term technical assistance.

OPERATIONS & SYSTEMS

During the first six months, DAI will also focus on establishing operating systems for the WALIS team include the Grants Manual, Performance Monitoring Plan, Field Operations Manual and our "Technical and Administrative Management Information System" or TAMIS. TAMIS is a secure database that is customized to meet each project's and client's needs while enforcing common compliance and management standards, TAMIS serves as a workflow management and reporting tool that integrates activity management, project administration, impact and performance monitoring, and streamlines subcontract and grant management along with other management tasks.

DRAFT SIX MONTH WORK PLAN SCHEDULE

Task	WALIS Lead Staff Member	2015 W1	W2	W3	W4	Nov	Dec	2016 Jan	Feb	Mar
Start-Up/Administrative Activities										
Meet with USAID TO COR and CO to review WALIS contract	COP and PM	◆								
Submit 30 day Action Plan	COP									
Recruit and mobilize WALIS Long Term US-based Team	COP and PM									
Recruit and mobilize Sr. Program Director (SPD) based in Africa	COP and PM									
Procure office equipment and install TAMIS	DAI Home Office									
Organize/hold kickoff meeting with USAID Staff and WALIS team	COP, SOM, TAM					◆				
Draft WALIS Information materials for USAID review	COP									
Organize and carry out WALIS Road Show (3 weeks)	COP, COR, SPD							◆	◆	
Submit Grants Manual to USAID for approval	COP and SOM				▲					
Reports/Deliverables										
Weekly check-in with COR and/or weekly email updates	COP and PM	▲	▲	▲	▲	▲	▲	▲	▲	▲
Submit first annual work plan (due 30 days following Award)	COP and PM			▲	▲					
Submit PMP (due 60 days following Award)	COP and SOM					▲				◆
Monthly meeting with COR/implementation and financial reports	COP and SOM				◆	◆	◆	◆	◆	◆
Submit quarterly progress reports	COP and SOM						▲		▲	▲
Task 1: Develop, Monitor, and Analyze Sound Sector Data										
Collect information on national monitoring and reporting systems during WALIS Roadshow	COP, SPD and M&E							◆	●	
Design and carry out workshops with AMCOW and AfWA staff to strengthen information provided through their website:	KM and STTA									◆
Follow-up STTA to Improve AMCOW and AfWA websites	STTA									↑
Initial outreach to at least two donors to establish collaborative approach to improving WASH data and analysis.	COP and SPD							◆	◆	◆
Task 2: Engage in Targeted Research and Pilot Activities Around Identified Sector Constraints										
Determine interest/need for a Research-On-Demand facility established/supported by WALIS at kickoff meeting with USAID	COP, SOM					◆				
Establish Research-on-Demand facility (if needed)	COP and KM							●		
Identify initial priorities for research, pilot and demonstration activities in consultation with USAID and regional organizations	COP and SPD									●
Evaluate replication/continuity of FABRI activities	COP and TAM									◆
Task 3: Strengthen Country Systems to Develop Informed Policy and Engage in Sector Planning Toward Sustainable Services										
Evaluate the JSR or similar process in at least two (2) countries	M&E and STTA								●	●
Identify high priority WASH issues that countries have in common	COP and M&E									↑
Task 4: Increase the Capacity Required to Support Improved Collection and Use of Sector Knowledge										
Launch first phase of training for guided self-assessments with AMCOW, AfWA, and ANEW	ISSSTTA								◆	◆

20 WATER FOR AFRICA THROUGH LEADERSHIP AND INSTITUTIONAL SUPPORT (WALIS)
SIX MONTH WORKPLAN

	= Ongoing Activity	**COP**	= Chief of Party	**SOM**	= Sr. Operations Manager
↑	= Activity that continues beyond six months	**ISS**	= Institutional Strengthening Specialist	**SPD**	= Sr. Program Director (based in Africa)
◀	= Deliverable	**KM**	= Knowledge Mgt Specialist	**STTA**	= Short-Term Technical Assistance
◆	= Key Meeting	**M&E**	= M&E Specialist	**TAM**	= Technical Activity Manager
●	= Report	**PM**	= Home Office Program Manager		